DK EYEWITNESS WORKBOOKS
Earth

by Caryn Jenner

Educational Consultants Linda B. Gambrell and Geraldine Taylor

Senior Editors Jane Yorke, Fleur Star
Senior Art Editor Owen Peyton Jones
Project Editors Jilly MacLeod, Sue Malyan
Editor Nayan Keshan
US Editor Lori Cates Hand
Art Editors Tanisha Mandal, Sara Nunan, Rebecca Painter, Peter Radcliffe, Susan St. Louis
DK Picture Library Claire Bowers, Rose Horridge
Managing Editors Christine Stroyan, Shikha Kulkarni
Managing Art Editors Anna Hall, Govind Mittal
DTP Designer Anita Yadav
Production Editor Tom Morse
Production Controller Nancy-Jane Maun
Senior Jacket Designer Suhita Dharamjit
Jacket Design Development Manager Sophia MTT
Publisher Andrew Macintyre
Art Director Karen Self
Publishing Director Jonathan Metcalf

This American Edition, 2020
First American Edition, 2007
Published in the United States by DK Publishing
1450 Broadway, Suite 801, New York, NY 10018

A catalog record for this book
is available from the Library of Congress.
ISBN: 978-0-7440-3451-6

DK books are available at special discounts when purchased in bulk for promotions, premiums, fund-raising, or educational use. For details, contact: DK Publishing Special Markets, 1450 Broadway, Suite 801, New York, NY 10018 or SpecialSales@dk.com

Printed and bound in Canada

For the curious

www.dk.com

Contents

Fast Facts

Activities

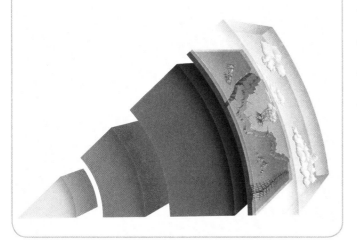

Quick Quiz

How This Book Can Help Your Child

Eyewitness Workbooks offer a fun and colorful range of stimulating titles on the subjects of history, science, and geography. Devised and written with the expert advice of educational consultants, each workbook aims to

- develop a child's knowledge of a popular topic
- provide practice of key skills and reinforce classroom learning
- nurture a child's special interest in a subject

About This Book

Eyewitness Workbook Earth is an activity-packed exploration of our planet and the forces that shape it. Inside you will find:

Fast Facts

This section presents key information as concise facts that are easy to digest, learn, and remember. Encourage your child to start by reading through the valuable information in the Fast Facts section and studying the statistics chart at the back of the book before trying out the activities.

Activities

The enjoyable fill-in activities are designed to develop information recall and help your child practice cross-referencing skills. Each activity can be completed using information provided on the page, in the Fast Facts section, or in the charts at the back of the book.

Quick Quiz

There are six pages of multiple-choice questions to test your child's newfound knowledge of the subject. Children should try answering the quiz questions only after all of the activity section has been completed.

Important Information

- Stress to your child the need to be careful when rock collecting. Make sure children take special care near water, stay away from clifftops and other dangerous places, and check tide times when rock collecting on the coast. Ideally, an adult should accompany children on their rock-collecting trips.

- It is not advisable to go rock collecting after heavy rain or strong winds.
- Children should wear sensible walking shoes or boots when rock collecting and, in cold or wet weather, warm, weather-proof clothing. They should take a map and a bottle of water, as well as a sturdy bag for carrying their rocks.

PROGRESS CHART

Chart your progress as you work through the activity and quiz pages in this book. First check your answers, then color in a star in the correct box below.

Page	Topic	Star	Page	Topic	Star	Page	Topic	Star
14	Earth time	☆	24	Rock collecting	☆	34	Weather watching	☆
15	Up in the air	☆	25	Rock collecting	☆	35	Weather watching	☆
16	Earth forces	☆	26	Oceans and seas	☆	36	Conserving Earth's resources	☆
17	Powerful plates	☆	27	Oceans and seas	☆	37	Conserving Earth's resources	☆
18	Erupting Earth	☆	28	Flowing rivers	☆	38	Earth and its structure	☆
19	World peaks	☆	29	Disappearing lakes	☆	39	Mountains, volcanoes, and earthquakes	☆
20	Amazing Earth	☆	30	Underground water	☆	40	Rocks, minerals, and soil	☆
21	Amazing Earth	☆	31	Ice and glaciers	☆	41	Earth, water, and ice	☆
22	Types of rocks	☆	32	Habitats of the world	☆	42	Climate, seasons, and weather	☆
23	Rocky secrets	☆	33	Clouds and water	☆	43	Features, habitats, and resources	☆

Planet Earth

11/23/20

Our planet Earth is one of eight known planets that orbit (circle around) the star we call the Sun. Earth is near enough to the Sun to benefit from its heat and light, but not so near that the heat burns. As far as we know, Earth is the only planet that has both air and water—two vital elements needed for life to exist.

Spinning planet

As Earth orbits the Sun, it also rotates (spins) around an invisible line, called its axis. This rotation gives us day and night. The part of Earth that is turned toward the Sun has day, while the part that is turned away has night. Earth rotates toward the east, so the Sun always rises in the east and sets in the west.

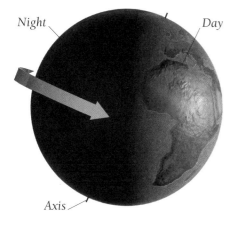

Night *Day*

Axis

Model of Earth spinning on its axis

Key facts

- Earth makes one complete rotation on its axis every 24 hours—that is, once a day.
- Earth makes one complete orbit of the Sun every 365.26 days—that is, once in just over a year.
- While Earth orbits the Sun, the Moon orbits Earth. The Moon makes one complete orbit every 27.3 days—about once a month.

Earth's atmosphere

The atmosphere is a blanket of gases that surrounds Earth. These gases trap the Sun's warmth and light, keeping temperatures on Earth's surface relatively steady. They also protect Earth from harmful rays from the Sun. The atmosphere is divided into four main layers, according to temperature.

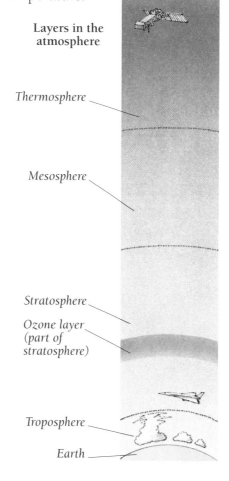

Layers in the atmosphere

Thermosphere

Mesosphere

Stratosphere

Ozone layer (part of stratosphere)

Troposphere

Earth

Life on Earth

We have air to breathe, water to drink, and a relatively mild climate. These conditions have allowed life to develop on Earth. The biosphere (the areas of Earth where life exists) is a varied place, with many different habitats. Each habitat is home to a huge diversity of life-forms.

Some of the many life-forms on Earth

Key facts

- The biosphere includes all of Earth's surface, the oceans, and the lower part of the atmosphere.
- A life-form is a thing that has the ability to grow, reproduce, and take in and use energy.
- Different kinds of life-forms include animals, plants, fungi such as yeast and mushrooms, and single-celled organisms such as bacteria.
- Experts think there are about 5 to 8 million different species (types) of insects—more than all other life-forms put together.
- Living things can evolve (change) over time to adapt to changes in the environment. However, scientists estimate that at least one species per day becomes extinct as a result of human activity.

11/23/20

Earth's Structure

During Earth's formation, heavy materials sank to the center of the planet, while lighter materials floated to the surface. Three main layers developed. In the center is a dense core of hot metal. This is surrounded by a thick, rocky mantle, which in turn is covered by a relatively thin crust—which is where we live.

Core

Earth's center is divided into the inner and outer cores. The inner core is a solid, red-hot ball that consists mainly of the heavy metals iron and nickel. Immense pressures stop these hot metals from melting. The outer core is made of liquid iron and nickel.

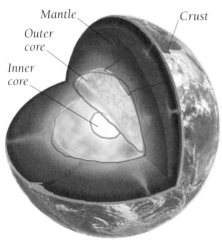

Mantle
Outer core
Inner core
Crust

Earth's structure

Key facts

- The center of Earth is about 4,000 miles (6,400 km) below the surface of the planet.
- The temperature in the solid inner core is 9,000–11,700°F (5,000–6,600°C). In the liquid outer core it is 7,200–10,800°F (4,000–6,000°C).
- Swirling liquid iron in the outer core generates a magnetic field around Earth.

Mantle

The mantle is divided into the upper and lower mantles. The lower mantle, which borders the outer core, is solid rock. The upper mantle is made of slowly moving, semisolid rock.

Key facts

- The mantle is 1,770 miles (2,850 km) deep and makes up 84 percent of Earth's volume.
- High pressures in the lower mantle keep the rock solid.
- Heat from the outer core causes currents in the mantle, which rise as hot material, then fall again as the material cools.
- The temperature in the lower mantle is 4,000–7,200°F (2,200–4,000°C). In the upper mantle it is less than 4,000°F (2,200°C).

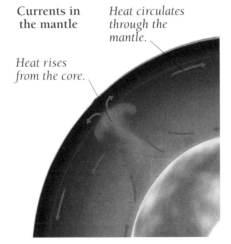

Currents in the mantle

Heat circulates through the mantle.

Heat rises from the core.

Crust

The uppermost layer of Earth's structure is the crust. It is made of huge pieces of rock, called tectonic plates, which cover Earth's surface. The plates float on a soft layer of molten (melted) mantle rock. Oceanic crust lies beneath the oceans. Continental crust lies under the land surface.

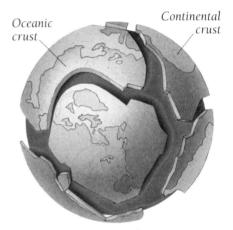

Oceanic crust

Continental crust

Tectonic plates

Key facts

- There are seven large tectonic plates and about 40 smaller ones.
- Continental crust is 16–45 miles (25–70 km) thick. Oceanic crust is thinner, and is only 4–7 miles (6–11 km) thick.
- Oceanic crust forms more than two-thirds of Earth's surface. It is made mostly of a volcanic rock called basalt, covered with a thin layer of sand and other sediments.
- Continental crust is made up of a variety of rocks. It is lighter than oceanic crust.
- Continental crust is deepest under young mountain ranges, such as the Himalayas.
- The boundary between Earth's crust and the mantle is called the Moho.

11/23/20

Violent Earth

The tectonic plates that form Earth's crust are constantly moving. They pull apart (diverge), push together (collide), and slide past each other. These movements create tall mountains, wide rift valleys, and deep ocean trenches. The moving plates also cause dramatic events, such as earthquakes and volcanic eruptions.

Mountains

Mountain ranges form when tectonic plates either collide or pull apart. The pressure caused by this movement makes layers of rock fracture and fold, and moves blocks of crust up or down. Fold mountains are tall and rugged. Block mountains have flat tops.

Mount Robson, Canada

Key facts

- The highest, most rugged mountain ranges are usually the youngest.
- Some young mountain ranges are still growing, as pressure keeps pushing rock layers up.
- Weathering and erosion wear down mountain peaks, so they eventually become gentler slopes.

Volcanoes

Melted, liquid

Hot molten rock in Earth's mantle is called magma. It collects in magma chambers. The pressure underground sometimes grows so great that the magma erupts through Earth's crust to form a volcano. Volcanoes most often occur along the edges of tectonic plates, where magma is most likely to form. Many volcanoes are situated under the oceans.

Key facts

- Magma emerges from a volcano in the form of lava.
- About 80 percent of the rock on Earth's surface is from volcanoes.
- Many volcanoes are situated along the edges of the Pacific plate, in an area called the Ring of Fire.

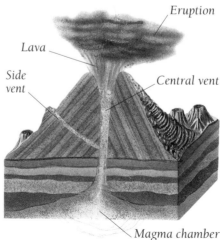

Eruption

Lava

Side vent

Central vent

Magma chamber

Cross-section through a volcano

Earthquakes

When tectonic plates push past each other, they create faults, or cracks, in the Earth's crust. Friction can make the rocks on either side of the fault stick rather than slide. Massive forces then build up underground until suddenly the rocks fracture, causing an earthquake.

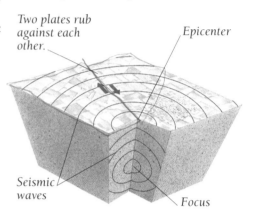

Two plates rub against each other.

Epicenter

Seismic waves

Focus

How earthquakes happen

Key facts

- Like volcanoes, earthquakes usually occur along the edges of tectonic plates.
- The point underground where the rocks fracture and cause the earthquake is called the focus.
- Vibrations called seismic waves ripple outward from the focus.
- The force of an earthquake is greatest on the surface of the Earth, directly above the focus. This point is called the epicenter.
- The magnitude (force) of an earthquake is measured on the Richter scale. The most powerful earthquakes measure about 9 on this scale.
- Some earthquakes are barely felt. Others are so strong that they can topple buildings and destroy whole cities.

Rocks and Minerals

Earth's crust is made of rocks. Rocks can be found in every part of Earth's surface, often covered by soil or water. Rocks are made of solid, naturally occurring materials called minerals. Different kinds of rocks are made from different combinations of minerals. Rocks are classified (grouped) according to how they formed.

Rocks

There are three types of rock. Igneous rocks have melted and then hardened. Sedimentary rocks form when particles of other rocks or sand are pressed together. Metamorphic rocks have been changed by heat or pressure. Rocks can change from one type to another.

Key facts

- Many sedimentary rocks form on the ocean floor or on a riverbed.
- Intrusive igneous rocks form when magma solidifies (hardens) underground.
- Extrusive igneous rocks form when lava cools outside a volcano.

Types of rock

Granite (igneous)

Breccia (sedimentary)

Marble (metamorphic)

Minerals

If you closely examine a rock under a magnifying glass or microscope, you will see tiny crystals. These are the minerals that make up the rock. Although there are more than 5,500 known minerals, only a few of them form the majority of the rocks found in Earth's crust.

Examples of minerals

Quartz with visible crystals

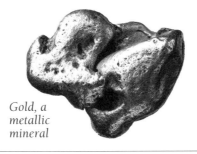

Gold, a metallic mineral

Key facts

- A mineral can be identified by certain characteristics, such as the shape of the crystals that it forms.
- Minerals include precious metals, such as gold and silver, and gemstones, such as diamonds and rubies.

Soil

Much of the continental crust has a layer of soil on top of the rock. Soil is made up of rock particles, minerals, air, water, and organic matter. This organic matter comes from the plants, animals, fungi, and bacteria that live in the soil. Plants take nutrients (food) and water from soil in order to grow.

Key facts

- Organic matter in the soil is called humus. It is made up largely of decayed plants and animals.
- When plants and animals die, millions of tiny creatures and bacteria in the soil break them down until they are recycled back into the soil.
- Soil acts as a filter for the water that enters rivers and lakes.
- Soil is made of different layers of material, from a rocky base called the bedrock, to upper layers of topsoil and humus.

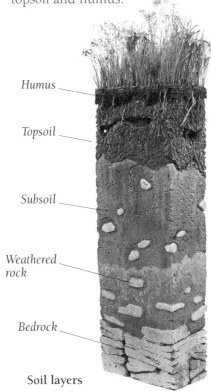

Humus

Topsoil

Subsoil

Weathered rock

Bedrock

Soil layers

Oceans

More than 70 percent of Earth's surface is covered by saltwater, in the form of oceans. The five oceans in order of size are the Pacific, Atlantic, Indian, Southern, and Arctic. Areas of water around the edges of the oceans that are partly enclosed by land are called seas. Salt in the oceans comes from dissolved minerals.

Ocean currents

Water is constantly moving through the world's oceans, in the form of currents. Cold polar water sinks to the depths of the ocean and flows toward the Equator (an imaginary line around the middle of Earth). Here, the tropical Sun warms the surface waters, which then move poleward, and are replaced by cooler water rising from depth.

→ Warm currents

⤳ Cold currents

Surface currents, caused by the wind

Key facts

- Surface currents are driven by the wind, which is influenced by Earth's rotation.
- Deep-water currents move very slowly, influenced by changes in the density of the water.
- The Gulf Stream is a warm ocean current that flows across the Atlantic to northwest Europe. It helps warm the local climate.

Ocean tide

Tides are a rise and fall of the oceans caused mainly by the pull of gravity between Earth and the Moon (gravity is a force that attracts all objects together). The effect causes bulges in the oceans. As Earth spins, these bulges move over the ocean surface, causing high and low tides.

A beach at low tide

Key facts

- Tides are most obvious at the coast.
- There are usually two high tides and two low tides each day.
- Twice a month, the Earth, Moon, and Sun are in line, creating extra gravitational pull. This causes a strong spring tide.
- Twice a month, the Earth, Moon, and Sun are at right angles to each other, causing a weak neap tide.

Waves

Wind blowing across the surface of the ocean causes the water to form waves. In areas where the wind is blowing, the ocean surface is choppy and chaotic. As water moves away from the windy area, it forms into waves. When they reach the coast, the waves break on the shore. Crashing waves erode rocks. They gradually reshape the coastline and create pillars, arches, and other interesting features.

Key facts

- The water in a wave appears to be moving forward, but it is actually moving in little circles.
- The circular movement of the water is greatest at the ocean's surface. Lower down, the water hardly moves at all.
- The highest point of a wave is called the crest. The lowest point is the trough.
- When a wave reaches the coast, it becomes too shallow for the water to move in circles, so the wave breaks on the shore.
- Waves often strike the shore diagonally. These waves carry sediment from the beach, such as sand and shingle, and drop it farther up the coast. This is called longshore drift.

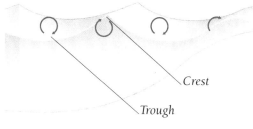

Crest

Trough

Ocean waves, showing circular movement of water

Rivers and Lakes

Rivers and lakes hold only a tiny fraction of all the water on Earth, but they have a vital role to play. Rivers and lakes provide an inland supply of fresh (not salty) water, irrigating (watering) the land, while also eroding it and carrying away the sediment. Rivers and lakes also collect rainfall that runs off the land.

Rivers

A river's course begins in the mountains, where rain and melted snow form a stream that flows rapidly down the steep slopes. The swiftly flowing water erodes the surrounding rock. As the landscape flattens out, the river slows and meanders (bends), depositing some of the sediment from upriver. The river's course ends at the sea.

Key facts

- The start of a river is called its source. The end of a river, where it meets the sea, is its mouth.
- A tributary is a smaller stream or river that flows into a main river.
- Rivers shape the landscape, carving out valleys and gorges, and carrying sediment downriver toward the sea.

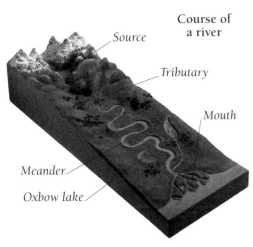

Course of a river

Source

Tributary

Mouth

Meander

Oxbow lake

Lakes

A lake is an inland body of water that has collected in a hollow. Hollows are formed by glaciers, volcanoes, river erosion, fault lines, or other movements of Earth. Over time, they fill with water from rivers, rain, or melting glaciers. Eventually, though, lakes either fill up with sediment or dry up and disappear.

Lakes on the Isle of Skye, Scotland, formed by glaciers

Key facts

- Most lakes contain fresh water, although some contain saltwater.
- A caldera lake is a volcanic crater that has filled with water.
- An oxbow lake forms from the curve of a meandering river.
- Glaciers and melted ice form kettle lakes, moraine lakes, and tarns.
- A tarn forms in a cirque—a bowl-shaped hollow at the head of a valley, left when a glacier melts.

Ice and glaciers

A glacier is a slow-moving river of ice. Glaciers are generally found in the polar regions and on high mountains. They cover about one-tenth of Earth's land surface and hold about three-quarters of all the world's fresh water. As a glacier flows slowly downhill, its huge weight presses on the rock beneath, eroding or carving out the landscape.

Key facts

- A glacier is formed from snow that is gradually compressed to become a dense mass of ice.
- As a glacier flows slowly down a mountain valley, it shifts rocks and debris in its path, forming heaps and ridges called moraines.
- Ice around the South Pole sits on land, while ice around the North Pole floats on water.
- An iceberg is part of a glacier that has broken off and fallen into the sea. About 90 percent of icebergs are found around Antarctica.

Gravity slowly moves a glacier down the valley.

Climate

The typical weather in a place is known as its climate. In general, the nearer a place is to the Equator, the hotter it is likely to be. Also, the higher up a place is, the colder and wetter it is likely to be. Inland areas are drier than coastal areas, because oceans create moisture that falls as rain on or near the coast.

Climate zones

Earth can be divided into five broad climate zones: tropical, dry, warm temperate, cool temperate, and polar. Within each zone, the weather can vary, but the climate tends to follow the same general pattern each year.

Key facts

- Tropical regions near the Equator tend to be hot and humid (damp).
- Dry areas are generally located inland, away from the oceans.
- Warm temperate regions have hot, dry summers and mild, wet winters.
- Cool temperate regions have plenty of rainfall year round, with cold, harsh winters.
- Polar regions are cold with crisp, dry air.

Equator

Climate zones

- Warm temperate
- Cool temperate
- Tropical
- Dry
- Polar

Habitats

A habitat is the environment in which a plant or animal lives. Different habitats support different kinds of life-forms. The plants and animals that live in tropical forests are different from those in polar regions.

Varied habitats on Earth

Key facts

- Tropical forests are home to more than 40 percent of all the plant and animal species on Earth.
- In deserts, high temperatures and dry winds dry up any moisture.
- Temperate regions have distinct seasons, so plants and animals must adapt to changing conditions during the year.
- Polar regions are dry. The ice does not evaporate, so there is little moisture in the air.

Seasons

Seasons occur because, as Earth orbits the Sun, its axis is slightly tilted. This means that different parts of the world get different amounts of sunlight throughout the year. For example, when the North Pole tilts toward the Sun, the Northern Hemisphere (the northern half of the globe) gets more sunlight, and it is summer. At the same time, the South Pole tilts away from the Sun, so the Southern Hemisphere gets less sunlight, and it is winter.

Key facts

- The Northern and Southern Hemispheres always have opposite seasons.
- The Sun sits high in the sky in summer, but low in winter.
- The Sun is at its highest point in the sky a few weeks into summer (called the summer solstice), and at its lowest point a few weeks into winter (the winter solstice).
- Spring and autumn occur when the Sun sits between its highest and lowest points in the sky.
- The Equator always faces the Sun, so it always gets plenty of sunlight. Areas near the Equator are hot and sunny year round.

Earth's annual orbit around the Sun

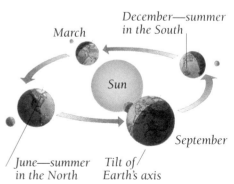

December—summer in the South

March

Sun

September

June—summer in the North

Tilt of Earth's axis

Weather

What is it like outside? Is it hot or cold? Sunny or rainy? These day-to-day conditions are what we mean by the term "weather." Heat from the Sun causes Earth's atmosphere to be in constant motion. As air and water move around in the atmosphere, they cause our changing weather conditions.

Winds

Wind is the movement of air caused by constant changes of temperature and pressure in the atmosphere. Winds are influenced by Earth's spin, which pushes air masses to the right in the Northern Hemisphere and to the left in the Southern Hemisphere. Winds are named after the direction from which they blow.

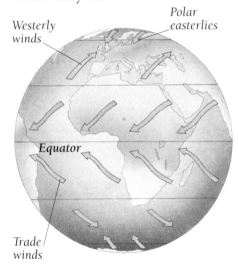

Westerly winds

Polar easterlies

Equator

Trade winds

Prevailing winds

Key facts

- In many places, the wind blows mostly from one particular direction. This is called the prevailing wind.
- The force of the wind is measured on the Beaufort Scale. Force 0 is completely calm, while Force 12 is a hurricane-force wind.

Clouds

Clouds form when water from lakes, rivers, and oceans evaporates (turns from liquid to gas) to become water vapor. As the water vapor rises, it cools and condenses (turns from gas to liquid) to become tiny water droplets or ice crystals. These gather to form clouds, which can release rain. This process is called the water cycle.

Key facts

- Clouds are classified into different types according to how they have formed and how high they are in the sky.
- Fog and mist are cloud that forms at ground level.

Cumulus—heaped clouds

Cirrus—wispy clouds

Rain

If there are enough water droplets in a cloud, they will fall as rain. Ice crystals in a cloud can melt as they fall and also form rain. Rainfall replaces water that has evaporated from Earth's surface, a vital part of the water cycle.

Key facts

- It takes about 3,000 droplets of water to form a light drizzle drop.
- About two million water droplets make one raindrop.
- Different places in the world have different levels of rainfall. The highest rainfall is in the tropics.

Rain makes life on Earth possible.

Snow and hail

When the air is cold, ice crystals in the clouds stick together to form snowflakes. Hailstones form when ice crystals are blown around inside the cloud, building up many frozen layers to become solid ice.

Snowflake

Key facts

- The heaviest snows fall when the temperature is just below freezing.
- Snowflakes always have six sides.
- Hailstones can be pea-sized, or as large as a grapefruit.

Earth Time

During the course of a complete orbit of the Sun, Earth rotates on its axis 365.26 times. This means that one year equals 365.26 days. But in our calendar we round this down to 365 days in a year, so every fourth year we add an extra day to enable us to synchronize (match up) with Earth's orbit. We call this a leap year.

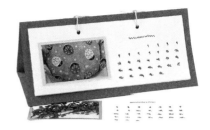

Calendars are based on Earth's movement around the Sun.

Time test

Circle the correct word to complete each sentence. Use the information on this page and on page 6 to help you.

1. Earth takes one year to orbit the **Moon / Sun**.

2. The rotation of the **Moon / Earth** gives us day and night.

3. The Sun rises in the **east / west**.

4. One complete **rotation / orbit** of Earth equals one day.

5. The **Moon / Sun** takes 27.3 days to orbit Earth.

6. Every four years, we have a leap year with **364 / 366** days.

Season facts

- In many parts of the world, Earth's orbit of the Sun creates a cycle of seasons.

- The longest day of the year is the summer solstice. The shortest is the winter solstice.

- During summer at the North and South Poles, the Sun shines continuously, both day and night. But in winter, there is no sunlight at all.

Which season?

Read the statements below about the seasons. Then number the pictures 1 to 4 to match them up with the right statements. Use the information on page 12 and in the fact box above to help you.

1. When it is fall in the Southern Hemisphere, it is this season in the Northern Hemisphere.

2. The Sun is at its lowest point during this season.

3. The longest day of the year occurs during this season.

4. This season follows summer.

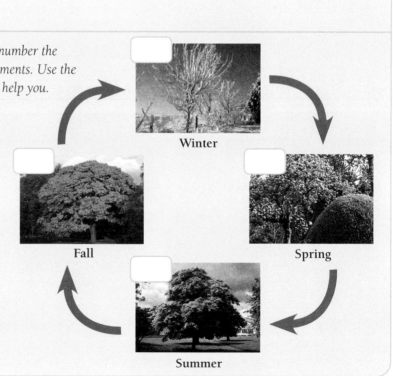

Winter

Spring

Fall

Summer

Up in the Air

The atmosphere is kept in place around Earth by gravity. It is divided into layers, and contains the gases oxygen and carbon dioxide, which animals and plants need to survive. The atmosphere also contains water vapor—another gas crucial to life—plus a thin layer of ozone gas, which helps protect us from the Sun's rays.

Atmospheric layers

Number the captions below 1 to 4, to match them up with the atmospheric layers shown in the diagram. Use the information on page 6 to help you.

Troposphere
We live in the troposphere, where most of the gases needed for life are found. Weather occurs in this layer. Water vapor gathers in clouds, then falls to Earth as rain or snow.

Thermosphere
Gases in this outer layer decrease until the atmosphere merges with space. Satellites and spectacular light displays, called auroras, may be found here.

Stratosphere
Jet airliners and weather balloons often fly here, above the clouds. A layer of ozone absorbs the Sun's harmful rays.

Mesosphere
This layer contains very little water vapor.

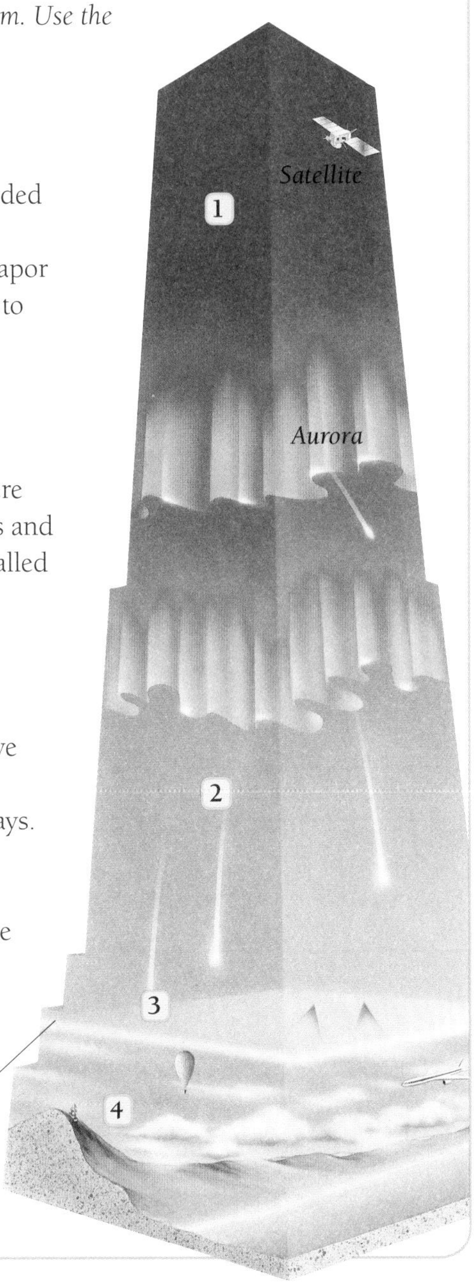

Satellite

Aurora

1

2

3

4

Ozone layer

Ozone layer facts

- The ozone layer acts as a screen, preventing harmful ultraviolet rays from the Sun from reaching Earth.
- Scientists have detected a hole in the ozone layer above the South Pole.
- Pollutants that reduce the ozone layer, such as CFCs (chemicals found in aerosol cans and refrigerator coolants), are now banned.
- Scientists hope that the ozone layer may repair itself by 2050. This will only happen if further damage is prevented.

True or false?

Read the following sentences about the atmosphere. Then, using the information on this page and page 6, check the boxes to show which facts are true or false.

	TRUE	FALSE
1. We live in the troposphere.	☐	☐
2. The mesosphere merges with space.	☐	☐
3. Weather occurs in the thermosphere.	☐	☐
4. Ozone protects Earth's surface from harmful ultraviolet rays.	☐	☐
5. The hole in the ozone layer is above the North Pole.	☐	☐
6. The ozone layer is in the stratosphere.	☐	☐

Earth Forces

Forces such as heat, pressure, and gravity are all at work on Earth, from the inner core to the outer atmosphere. In the crust, powerful forces cause the tectonic plates to move. Scientists think Earth's continents were once joined together, but that they gradually drifted apart as tectonic plates shifted. This is called continental drift.

Map of Earth, showing the major tectonic plates

Inside the Earth

Write the name of each part of Earth's structure in the spaces below, matching them to the numbers on the picture. Use the information on page 7 to help you. Choose from:

crust   atmosphere   outer core   mantle   inner core

1 ....

2 ....

3 ....

4 ....

5 ....

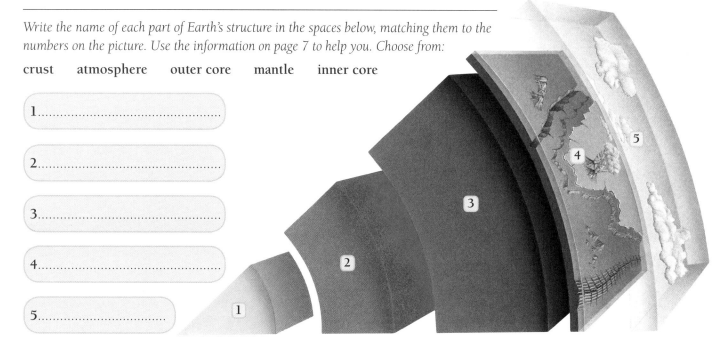

Tectonic jigsaw puzzle

Read the tectonic plate facts on page 17. Then, using the map at the top of the page, color in the tectonic plates on the map, making sure the land is green and the sea is blue.

KEY

☐ Divergent boundary

■ Convergent boundary

■ Transform fault

- - - Uncertain

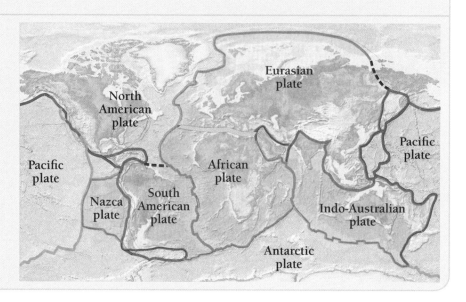

Powerful Plates

Tectonic plates move very slowly, but their effects are enormous. Plate movements affect Earth's crust in dramatic ways, especially where two plates meet at plate boundaries. As plates pull apart or collide, mountains form, volcanoes erupt, and earthquakes shake the land.

Which boundary?

Complete each sentence by writing in the correct type of plate boundary, using information in the fact box on the right. Choose from:

divergent boundary   **convergent boundary**   **transform fault**

1. Two plates slide past each other in a ....

2. Two plates pull apart in a ....

3. Two plates collide in a ....

4. An earthquake is caused by a ....

Tectonic plate facts

Divergent boundary
When two plates pull apart, blocks of land fall into the gap. Molten rock may then rise through the gap, forming new crust.

Convergent boundary
When two plates collide, one plate is pushed under the other. Some crust in the upper plate melts, often rising again as a volcano.

Transform fault
When two plates slide past each other, friction may cause them to stick. They eventually become unstuck with a violent jolt, causing an earthquake.

Measuring earthquakes

The Mercalli scale measures an earthquake based on the effects it causes. These pictures show the effects of three earthquakes. The red dots on the Mercalli scale indicate the measurement for each earthquake. Write the correct number from the Mercalli scale next to each picture.

a.

c.

b.

Mercalli scale

1 Vibrations detected by instruments

2 Vibrations felt by people

● 3 Hanging light bulbs sway

4 Plates and windows rattle

5 Buildings tremble, small objects move

● 6 Windows break, objects fall off shelves

7 Difficult to stand

8 Chimneys fall

9 Ground cracks

● 10 Buildings collapse

11 Landslides occur

12 Nearly total destruction

Erupting Earth

Volcanoes occur at divergent or convergent boundaries. When plates pull apart, a chain of relatively gentle eruptions may occur. But when plates collide, immense heat and pressure cause molten rock and clouds of ash to erupt in a violent explosion. Layers of ash and lava then pile up to form a volcanic mountain.

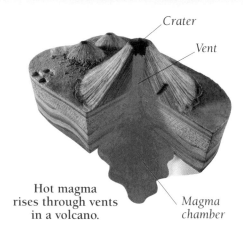

Crater
Vent

Hot magma rises through vents in a volcano.

Magma chamber

Fiery mountains

Fill in the missing words about volcanoes, using the information above and on page 8. Choose from: **lava   magma chamber   ash   vents**

1. Hot molten rock collects in the ....

2. Magma rises through the ....

3. Magma emerges from a volcano in the form of ....

4. Layers of .... and lava form a volcanic mountain.

Eruption facts

- A **volcanic crater** is a hollow that forms at the top of an erupted volcano.

- **Pahoehoe** is fluid lava that hardens into rope-shaped rock.

- **Obsidian** is a glassy volcanic rock formed from rapidly cooling lava.

- **Cinder cones** are small volcanoes, made of volcanic rock filled with gas bubbles.

Volcano picture puzzle

Label these pictures of rocks and land formations created by volcanic eruptions, using the descriptions in the fact box above.

1. ....

2. ....

3. ....

4. ....

World Peaks

Mountains are rock masses that tower above the surrounding landscape, forced up by movements in the Earth's crust. They make up about five percent of the land on Earth, and can be classified according to how they were formed. The three main types are volcanic mountains, fold mountains, and block mountains.

True or false?

Read the following sentences about mountains. Using the information on this page and page 8, check the boxes to show which facts are true or false.

	TRUE	FALSE
1. Mountains make up five percent of the land on Earth.	☐	☐
2. Block mountains form when rocks fold over.	☐	☐
3. Fold mountains have relatively flat peaks.	☐	☐
4. Weathering and erosion wear away mountains.	☐	☐
5. Older mountains generally have taller, sharper peaks than younger mountains.	☐	☐
6. Some fold mountains are still growing.	☐	☐

Mountain facts

Fold mountains
Heat and pressure, usually at convergent boundaries, can cause rocks deep in the crust to buckle up. Over time, the rocks fold into each other to form high peaks.

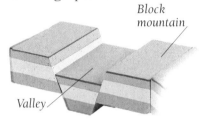

Block mountain

Valley

Block mountains
Movement in the Earth's crust, often at divergent boundaries, can push blocks of land upward or downward, creating mountains and valleys.

Mountain quiz

Use information on the charts at the back of the book to answer these questions. Then see if you can find the mountain ranges in an atlas.

1. What is the world's highest mountain? ....

2. Which mountain range is it in? ....

3. On which continent are the Atlas Mountains located? ....

4. What is the highest peak in the Alps? ....

5. How long is the Andes mountain range? ....

6. Which mountain range contains Mt. Elbert? ....

Mount Everest

Amazing Earth

There is an amazing variety of landscapes on our planet—from tropical forests and scorching deserts to vast oceans and icy wildernesses. These landscapes are formed over millions of years by processes, such as plate movements and erosion, that keep Earth constantly changing.

Natural wonders of the world

This map of the world shows some of the many spectacular landscapes on Earth. Fill in the names of the Earth record breakers from the chart at the back of the book.

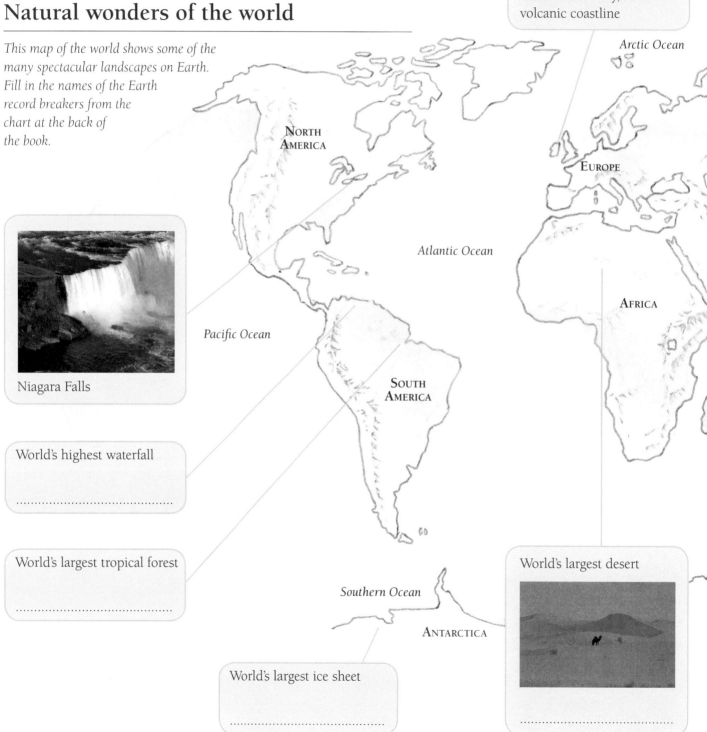

Giant's Causeway, a volcanic coastline

Arctic Ocean

NORTH AMERICA

EUROPE

Atlantic Ocean

AFRICA

Pacific Ocean

Niagara Falls

SOUTH AMERICA

World's highest waterfall

....

World's largest tropical forest

....

Southern Ocean

ANTARCTICA

World's largest desert

World's largest ice sheet

....

....

World's largest lake

....

The Antarctic ice sheet contains more than 60 percent of the world's fresh water. If it were to melt, much of Earth's land would become flooded.

Huang Shan, a beautiful mountain range

Pacific Ocean

ASIA

Indian Ocean

AUSTRALIA

World's largest ocean

....

Uluru (Ayers Rock), an enormous sandstone rock

Where you live

Look at a local map to learn about the natural wonders in your area. Then answer the following questions.

Name of **highest point** ....

Height ....

Name of **nearest river** ....

Source ....

River mouth ....

Name of **nearest sea** or **ocean**.

....

Type of coast (sandy beach / cliffs / gravel)

....

Distance from home ....

Check the boxes to show other geographical features found in your area.

Forest or woodland ☐

Lake or pond ☐

Waterfall ☐

Wetland or marshes ☐

Grassland ☐

Rock formations ☐

Cave ☐

Desert ☐

Types of rocks

When you look at a rock, it seems solid and unchanging. But rocks do change, over millions and sometimes billions of years. Forces such as heat, pressure, and erosion are constantly changing them from one type of rock to another. This endless process of change is called the rock cycle.

Rock cycle puzzle

Read these steps describing how rocks change in the course of the rock cycle. Then look carefully at the diagram below, and number the boxes to match up with each step in the cycle.

1. Igneous rocks form when lava from volcanoes cools and hardens above ground, or when magma cools and hardens below ground.

2. Weathering by ice, snow, wind, and water erodes all types of rocks, creating sediments (tiny rock particles) that are carried downhill.

3. Rivers carry the sediments toward the sea.

4. Layers of sediments build up on the seabed and harden to become sedimentary rock.

5. Heat and pressure deep underground change rocks of all types to form metamorphic rocks.

6. Rocks of all types melt to form magma. This may harden below ground, or be forced up to the surface as lava during a volcanic eruption.

Rocky landscapes

Read the captions below, then use the information on page 9 to help you name each type of rock being shown. Choose from:

igneous   sedimentary   metamorphic

1. Heat and pressure deep underground transformed the rocks that made up these ancient mountains. These are

....rocks.

2. This rock was created when magma solidified deep under the ground, then became exposed by erosion and weathering. This is

....rock.

3. Small particles of eroded rock hardened to form these rocky cliffs. These are

....rocks.

Rocky Secrets

By examining the characteristics of a rock, you can find clues to the identity of the minerals that make it up. Some sedimentary rocks may also contain traces of the ancient past, in the form of plants and animals that have turned into fossils.

Mineral test

Read the mineral facts opposite. Then circle the correct word to complete each sentence. Use the information in the mineral facts on the right to help you.

1. **Streak / color** is revealed by rubbing the mineral against an unglazed tile.

2. Transparency and luster relate to **light / hardness**.

3. The crystal system describes the **color / shape** of the crystals.

4. Cleavage and fracture describes how the mineral **looks / breaks**.

5. The hardest mineral is **gypsum / diamond**.

6. Calcite is **harder / softer** than quartz.

How fossils form

Number the pictures and captions 1 to 4 to show the order in which fossils form.

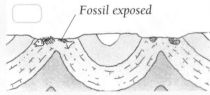
Fossil exposed

The fossils are eventually exposed on the Earth's surface, often embedded in the rock.

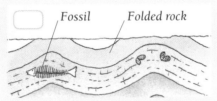
Fossil   Folded rock

Over time, the rock is folded by forces such as heat and pressure. The surface becomes eroded.

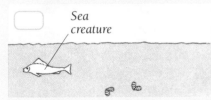
Sea creature

When sea creatures die, they sink to the seabed. The soft parts rot away, leaving only hard parts, such as bones, teeth, and shells.

Remains of sea creature   Rocks form

Layers of sediment bury the remains and harden to rock. Rock-forming minerals replace the original ones in the remains, which harden to fossils.

Mineral facts

Characteristics used to identify minerals include:

- **Crystal system**: the shape of the individual crystals
- **Color**: the color of the mineral
- **Streak**: the color you get when you rub the mineral against an unglazed tile
- **Cleavage** and **fracture**: how the mineral breaks apart
- **Transparency** and **luster**: how light passes through, or reflects off, the mineral
- **Hardness**: hardness of the mineral in comparison to other minerals

Mohs' scale—used to measure the hardness of a mineral

Hardest

10		Diamond
9		Corundum
8		Topaz
7		Quartz
6		Orthoclase
5		Apatite
4		Fluorite
3		Calcite
2		Gypsum
1		Talc

Softest

23

Rock Collecting

The best way to find out more about rocks is to start a rock collection of your own. On close inspection, you will soon discover that there are many different kinds of rocks to be found right in your local area.

Grain-size puzzle

A characteristic commonly used to identify rocks is the size of the small grains, or particles, in the rocks. Shown below are three sedimentary rocks that have been magnified under a microscope. Read the descriptions below, then identify what type of grain each rock has. Choose from: **coarse medium fine**

- **Coarse grains** can be seen with the naked eye.
- **Medium grains** can be seen with a magnifying glass.
- **Fine grains** can only be seen with a microscope.

Sandstone
Grain size:

Quartz conglomerate
Grain size:

Shale
Grain size:

1. ....

2. ....

3. ....

Identifying tips

- Igneous rocks usually have tightly interlocking crystals, so they are very hard.
- Sedimentary rocks often have a crumbly texture, sometimes with visible layers of sediment.
- The shape of the grains in a sedimentary rock indicates whether the sediment particles were transported by the wind or by water.
- Metamorphic rocks formed by heat and pressure may be foliated (have wavy bands running through them).
- Metamorphic rocks that are formed by heat alone are not foliated.

Match the rocks and minerals

Look at the pictures of the rocks and minerals below, then read the descriptions. Can you match the correct description with its picture?

1.

2.

3.

a. Chalk is pure limestone, without any additional minerals. It is a sedimentary rock, with fine white grains and a soft powdery texture.

b. Ruby is a variety of the mineral corundum. It is red or pink in color, and has a white streak. Ruby crystals are found inside this rock.

c. Gneiss is a metamorphic rock with coarse grains that form dark- and light-colored wavy bands. It is often found in mountain ranges.

Organizing your rock collection

As you build your rock collection, gather information about each rock specimen. Follow these steps to organize your rocks and the information.

1 After washing and drying your rock, paint a dab of correction fluid on the rock and let it dry. Then write a reference number on the dab.

2 Arrange your rocks in a box or drawer. Display your best specimens in small, separate boxes lined with tissue paper or cotton balls. Mineral shops sell special specimen boxes and trays.

3 Use a guidebook to identify the rocks in your collection. Then keep a record of each specimen, writing details on a card like the one shown below. Include the reference number written on the rock, and keep adding information as you learn more about your collection.

ROCK REFERENCE NUMBER: 24

Location found:	Gravel beach at Grand Haven
Appearance: (How the rock looks)	Sandy-colored, medium-sized grains, faint signs of layering
Texture: (How the rock feels)	Rough texture like sandpaper, a bit crumbly when rubbed
Likely type of rock:	Sedimentary
I think this rock is:	SANDSTONE

Rock-collecting tips

- Good places to hunt for rocks include fields, pebble beaches, riverbanks, lakesides, and at the bottom of cliffs. Always tell an adult where you are going, and beware of hazards (see page 5).

Cleaning a rock specimen

- Ask permission before rock hunting on private land or protected areas.
- Collect only loose rocks.
- Take a sturdy bag to carry your rock specimens in.
- Take photographs of the landscapes where you collect your rocks.
- When you get home, clean your rock specimens with warm water and a scrubbing brush. Then dry gently.

Did you know?

The most common igneous rock is called basalt, which makes up most of the world's ocean floor. A type of basalt has also been found on the Moon.

Basalt

4. **d. Galena** is a common mineral in rocks. It is dark gray in color with a shiny metallic luster and a cubic crystal system.

5. **e. Obsidian** is a glassy, dark-colored igneous rock with sharp edges and very fine grains. It is used to make surgical scalpel blades.

Oceans and Seas

The vast oceans that cover over 70 percent of our planet may look like unremarkable expanses of water, but beneath the surface lie features just as distinctive as those found on land. The deeper you go, the darker and colder it gets, yet plants and animals still thrive here.

On the ocean floor

Read these descriptions of some of the features that can be found on the ocean floor. Then fill in the missing labels on the diagram below.

- The **continental shelf** is an undersea ledge that extends from the edge of the land.
- The **continental slope** descends from the continental shelf to the abyssal plain.
- The **abyssal plain** is a flat area of sediment on the ocean floor.
- A **seamount** is an underwater volcano.

- A **spreading ridge** forms where hot magma rises up from deep underwater, between two diverging tectonic plates.
- A **guyot** is a flat-topped seamount.
- A long, **deep-sea trench** occurs where one tectonic plate descends beneath another, causing the ocean floor to sink into the mantle.

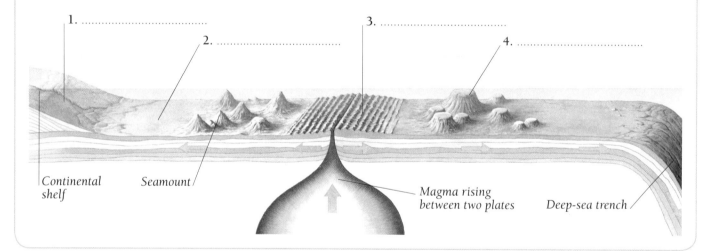

1. ....

2. ....

3. ....

4. ....

Continental shelf   *Seamount*   *Magma rising between two plates*   *Deep-sea trench*

Ocean quiz

Circle the correct answers to complete the statements below. Use the information on page 10 to help you.

1. In the ocean, cold water currents flow **toward / away from** the Equator.

2. The main cause of ocean tides is the gravitational pull between Earth and **Sun / Moon**.

3. The weakest tide is the **spring / neap** tide.

4. The highest point of a wave is called the **trough / crest**.

5. The circular movement of water in a wave is greatest at the ocean's **surface / floor**.

A wave

Ocean zones

The oceans are divided into zones, with each zone supporting its own range of wildlife. Draw the missing sea creatures in the correct zones on this diagram.

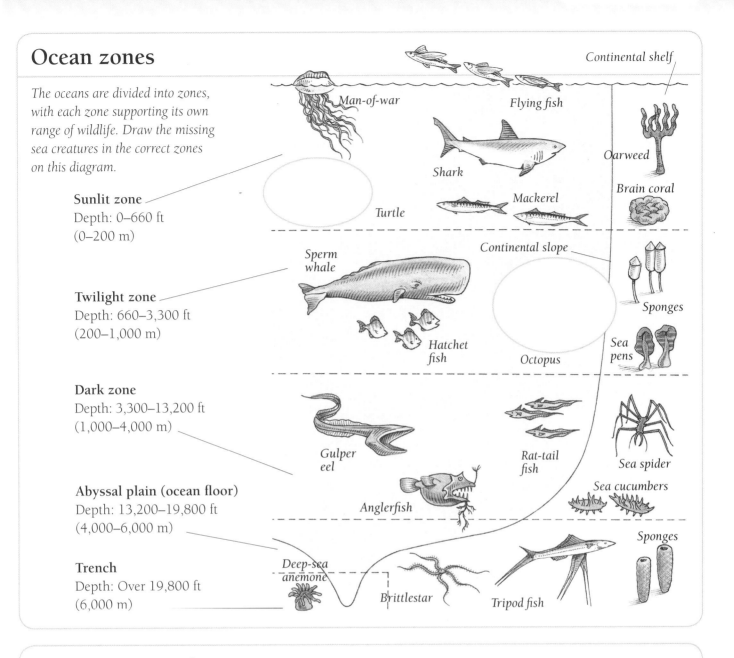

Sunlit zone
Depth: 0–660 ft
(0–200 m)

Twilight zone
Depth: 660–3,300 ft
(200–1,000 m)

Dark zone
Depth: 3,300–13,200 ft
(1,000–4,000 m)

Abyssal plain (ocean floor)
Depth: 13,200–19,800 ft
(4,000–6,000 m)

Trench
Depth: Over 19,800 ft
(6,000 m)

Man-of-war • Flying fish • Continental shelf • Shark • Oarweed • Brain coral • Mackerel • Turtle • Sperm whale • Continental slope • Hatchet fish • Octopus • Sponges • Sea pens • Gulper eel • Rat-tail fish • Sea spider • Anglerfish • Sea cucumbers • Deep-sea anemone • Brittlestar • Tripod fish • Sponges

Match the coastline

Coastlines occur where the oceans and seas meet the land. Read the captions below about different kinds of coastlines, then write the correct number against each picture.

1. Deposition
Waves deposit sand, creating a curved beach between two headlands.

2. Longshore drift
Waves hit the coastline at an angle, gradually moving the sand up the long beach.

3. Submergent coast
Melting glaciers cause the sea level to rise up the mountainous coastline.

4. Eroded coast
Waves and wind erode the cliffs, creating a jagged, rocky coastline.

Flowing Rivers

Between its narrow source and its wide mouth, a river is constantly changing. At any point along its course, the nature of a river depends on the slope of the landscape, the amount of water it is carrying, and the rocks that make up the riverbed and surrounding area.

A river runs broad and shallow through gently sloping land.

River features puzzle

Each of these photographs shows a river feature, as described below. Read the captions, then write the name of the correct feature under each picture.

A **waterfall** forms when the riverbed changes from hard rock to soft rock. The river erodes the soft rock, creating a sheer drop.

Meanders form when a river curves and loops its way across the flat lower levels of its course.

Rapids occur in the upper levels of the river as it flows swiftly downhill, cutting into the mountains.

A **floodplain** is a flat expanse of land beside the river that becomes covered with water whenever the river floods. Floodplains make fertile farmland.

1. ....

2. ....

3. ....

4. ....

Follow the rivers

Locate each of the rivers listed on the charts at the back of the book in a world map or atlas. Follow the course of each river from its source to its mouth. Then fill in this chart, stating whether the river flows north, south, east, or west from its source.

	Nile	Amazon	Volga
River source			
River mouth			
Flow direction			

Disappearing Lakes

The water that flows into a lake often carries with it a large amount of sediment that settles in the lake. The water volume drops as the sediment gradually fills the lake. Over time, new forms of plant life begin to grow, causing the lake area to get smaller and shallower. Eventually, the lake may dry up completely, or wetlands may form.

Did you know?

The deepest freshwater lake in the world is Lake Baikal in Russia, which plunges to a depth of 5,387 ft (1,642 m). This vast lake is home to about 2,000 unique species of plants and animals.

Lake formations

Circle the correct word to complete each statement. Use the information on page 11 to help you.

1. A lake is an **inland / coastal** body of water that has collected in a hollow.

2. **Tarns / caldera lakes** form in the craters of volcanoes.

3. **Oxbow / moraine** lakes are formed from a curve in a meandering river.

4. Kettle lakes, moraine lakes, and tarns are all types of lakes created by **glaciers / rivers**.

True or false?

Read the following sentences about wetlands. Using the information on this page, check the boxes to show which facts are true and which are false.

	TRUE	FALSE
1. A lake may gradually turn into a wetland.	☐	☐
2. As sediment fills a lake, the water volume rises.	☐	☐
3. A swamp is a type of wetland.	☐	☐
4. Wetlands often occur at a river delta.	☐	☐
5. Floodplains may become wetlands during the dry season.	☐	☐

Wetland facts

- Wetlands can be either freshwater or saltwater.
- Swamps, marshes, fens, and bogs are all types of wetlands.

- Wetlands often occur at a river delta, an area of sediment deposited at the mouth of a river. Here, seawater and freshwater become mixed together.

- River floodplains may become wetlands during the rainy season, when they become submerged in water.

Underground Water

Water exists below the surface of the land in the form of groundwater. Some rocks are impermeable, preventing water from seeping through. Other rocks are permeable, and hold groundwater like a sponge. A few rocks, such as limestone, are dissolved by water, forming holes that are gradually eroded to form tunnels and caves.

Did you know?

The world's deepest known cave is the Veryovkina Cave in Georgia, (on the border of Europe and Asia), which is 7,257 ft (2,212 m) deep. Scientists believe there may be other caves in the world, as yet unexplored, that are even deeper.

Inside a cave

Read the descriptions below of some of the features found in and around a cave.
Then number the diagram 1 to 7 to match up with these descriptions.

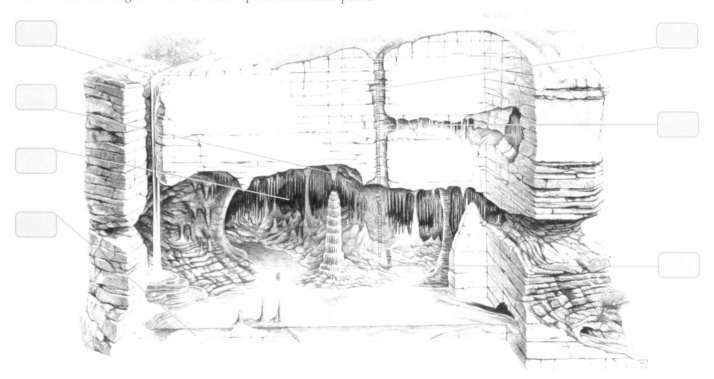

Cave features

1. A **sinkhole** is a hole in the surface rock that allows water to flow underground.

2. A **chimney** is a vertical opening in the rock.

3. A **gallery** is a large underground chamber.

4. A **water table** is the level at which the rock is saturated with water.

5. A **horizontal gallery** was formed when the water table was at a higher level.

6. A **stalactite** is a limestone deposit that hangs down from the roof of the cave.

7. A **stalagmite** is a limestone deposit that rises from the floor of the cave.

Inside a cave gallery

Ice and Glaciers

A glacier is made up of layers of snow that have been compressed to form thick rivers of ice. The world's largest glaciers are the massive ice sheets that cover the Antarctic. Much of the Arctic is also covered with ice. The huge size and weight of a glacier molds the land, creating distinctive features such as valleys and lakes.

Did you know?

Parts of the Antarctic ice sheet are over 2½ miles (4 km) thick. Some of the deeper ice in it is millions of years old.

The glacial landscape

Look closely at the pictures below, then complete each of these sentences using the information on this page and page 11 to help you.

1. A .... valley is formed by a huge, heavy glacier.

2. A lake that forms in a cirque, after a glacier melts, is a ....

3. A .... is a pile of rocks and debris that builds up along the sides and at the end of a glacier.

4. A tributary valley that is cut off by a deeper glacial valley is called a

....

A glacier and the landscape created after it melts

Arctic or Antarctic?

Use the information in the fact box below to answer the following questions. Choose from:

Arctic   Antarctic

1. Where is the South Pole?

....

2. Where is the North Pole?

....

3. Which region has land, covered by a huge ice sheet?

....

4. Where do polar bears live?

....

5. Where do penguins live?

....

Polar facts

The Arctic

• The Arctic surrounds the North Pole. It is largely ocean that is permanently covered in ice.

• Arctic land that is not ice-covered year round is called tundra, meaning "treeless plain."

• Polar bears live in the Arctic.

The Antarctic

• The Antarctic surrounds the South Pole. It is largely a frozen landmass called Antarctica.

• About 98 percent of Antarctica is covered by an immense ice sheet.

• Penguins, such as the emperor penguin, live in the Antarctic.

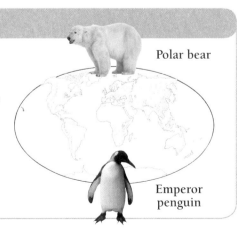

Polar bear

Emperor penguin

Habitats of the World

A habitat is largely shaped by climate. Other factors include the landscape of the area and the type of soil found there. Living things are well adapted to their own habitat, with physical characteristics and behavior that enable them to survive. A few life-forms, such as humans, can adapt to many different habitats.

Rivers and wetlands
Alligators and .... have eyes and nostrils on the top of their heads so they can see and breathe while they are ....

Animal adaptations

Look at the pictures of animals in their habitats and fill in the missing words in the captions. Choose from this list:

beaks   blubber   crocodiles   digesting   fat   fur   grassland
rainforest   sand   sheep   steep   swimming   tails   tree

Tropical forest
Monkeys use their long limbs and .... to swing from tree to tree in the tropical ....

Polar regions
Seals have an extra layer of .... called............ beneath their skin, which helps keep them warm.

Mountains
With their hooves and amazing agility, bighorn .... climb with ease up .... rocky mountainsides.

Desert
Desert hamsters have ..... on the soles of their feet to keep from burning as they jump across the hot ....

Temperate forest
Woodpeckers have strong, sharp .... that they use to drill nesting holes in .... trunks.

Grassland
Wildebeest are particularly good at .... grass, making them well adapted to their .... home.

Clouds and Water

Tiny particles of water vapor can hardly be seen or felt. But when the particles gather together they form clouds, which appear in a variety of formations in the sky. When enough particles gather, they form larger particles that fall to the ground as rain or snow.

The water cycle

Look carefully at this diagram of the water cycle. Then read the facts on the right, describing how water circulates between the Earth's surface and the atmosphere. Number the boxes on the diagram to correspond with each step in the water cycle.

Water cycle facts

1. Water evaporates from the oceans, lakes, and rivers to form clouds.
2. Clouds carry water inland.
3. Clouds release rain and snow onto the land.
4. Rivers carry water downhill toward the ocean.
5. Groundwater also flows toward the ocean.

Cloud puzzle

Read the descriptions of four main types of clouds.
Then write the correct type of cloud under each picture.

1..

2..

3..

4..

Stratus clouds form a sheet of low-lying cloud, often seen as mist or fog.

Cumulus clouds are fluffy white clouds, often seen on sunny days.

Cirrus clouds are wispy, high-altitude clouds made of ice crystals.

Cumulus clouds gather to form gray **cumulonimbus** rain clouds.

Weather Watching

Our weather is caused by the Sun's heat warming the air around us. As warm air rises, it creates areas of low pressure. Cold air sinks, creating areas of high pressure. Winds form when air rushes from high to low pressure areas. Forecasters predict what the weather will be like by studying air pressure and looking for patterns.

Wind force puzzle

The Beaufort scale measures the force of the wind from 0 to 12. Figure out the wind force shown in each of these pictures by reading the information in the box on the right, then write your answers in the space provided.

1.

2.

3.

4.

1. ....

2. ....

3. ....

4. ....

Measure the rainfall

Measure the rainfall where you live.

1 When you see rain clouds in the sky, place a clear container in an open space outside. Collect the rain, from as soon as it starts to fall until it stops.

2 Use a ruler to measure the amount of rainfall and record the result in your weather chart.

Beaufort scale

0 **Calm:** Wind speed 0.1 mph (0.2 kph). Air feels still. Smoke rises vertically.

1 **Light air:** Wind speed 2 mph (3 kph). Chimney smoke drifts gently.

2 **Light breeze:** Wind speed 5 mph (9 kph). Leaves rustle. Wind felt on face.

3 **Gentle breeze:** Wind speed 10 mph (15 kph). Leaves rustle. Flags flutter gently.

4 **Moderate breeze:** Wind speed 15 mph (25 kph). Leaves and paper blown around.

5 **Fresh breeze:** Wind speed 22 mph (35 kph). Small trees start to sway.

6 **Strong breeze:** Wind speed 28 mph (45 kph). Hard to control an umbrella.

7 **Near gale:** Wind speed 35 mph (56 kph). Whole trees sway.

8 **Gale:** Wind speed 42 mph (68 kph). Difficult to walk. Twigs broken off trees.

9 **Severe gale:** Wind speed 50 mph (80 kph). Shingles blown off. Branches broken.

10 **Storm:** Wind speed 58 mph (94 kph). Trees uprooted. Houses damaged.

11 **Severe storm:** Wind speed 68 mph (110 kph). Cars overturned.

12 **Hurricane:** Wind speed more than 73 mph (118 kph). Widespread damage.

Keep a weather chart

Observe the weather every day for a week and record your findings on this chart.

1 Every evening, check the weather forecast for the following day in your area. When you fill in your chart the next day, see if the weather forecast matches your findings.

2 Use your chart to see if you can detect patterns that help you to predict the weather. The following week, make your own weather forecasts for each day and see how accurate you are.

Day and date	Sunshine	Clouds	Precipitation (rain or snow)	Temperature	Wind force
Sample	AM – bright sun PM – partly sunny	Cumulus then cumulonimbus	Rainfull = 2.5 cm (1 in)	15°C (59°F) at 12.30 pm	Strong wind – force 6
Monday					
Tuesday					
Wednesday					
Thursday					
Friday					
Saturday					
Sunday					

Conserving Earth's Resources

Earth provides us with many resources, including water, trees, metals, and fossil fuels, to name a few. But these resources are not endless, and may run out if we do not conserve them. Another of Earth's precious resources is the atmosphere, which is being damaged by our use of fossil fuels, resulting in climate change across the globe.

Carbon facts

- Carbon dioxide occurs naturally in the atmosphere, helping keep Earth warm.
- Burning fossil fuels releases an excess of carbon dioxide into the atmosphere.
- Plants absorb carbon dioxide. But the destruction of forests means that less carbon dioxide is now being absorbed from the atmosphere.
- Too much carbon dioxide in the atmosphere causes unnatural changes to the world's climate, such as rising temperatures.
- Increasing temperatures cause sea levels to rise. If climate change continues, coastal areas and islands could eventually be submerged.

True or false?

Read the following sentences about climate change. Using the information on this page, check the boxes to show which facts are true and which are false.

	TRUE	FALSE
1. Plants absorb carbon dioxide from the atmosphere.	☐	☐
2. Increasing temperatures cause sea levels to drop.	☐	☐
3. Burning fossil fuels absorbs excess carbon dioxide.	☐	☐
4. Too much carbon dioxide causes unnatural changes to the world's climate.	☐	☐
5. Carbon dioxide occurs naturally in the atmosphere.	☐	☐

Fossil fuels puzzle

Oil and natural gas are types of fossil fuels. They were formed from dead organisms that were buried beneath layers of sediment millions of years ago. Today, we drill deep wells to extract these fossil fuels, which are used for heating our homes, producing electricity, or powering our cars. However, Earth's supply of fossil fuels is running low and cannot keep up with demand for much longer.

Read the captions below explaining how fossil fuels are formed, then number them in the right order.

- ☐ Over time, other rocks trap the oil and gas in underground reservoirs.
- ☐ Dead organisms fall to the ocean floor.
- ☐ Oil and gas push into the surrounding rock.
- ☐ Sediment compresses the remains of organisms to form oil and natural gas.

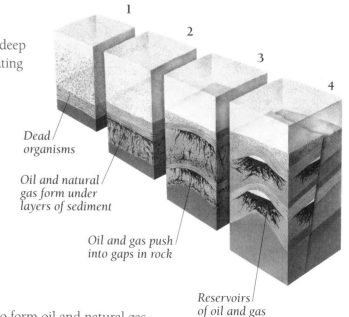

1 2 3 4

Dead organisms

Oil and natural gas form under layers of sediment

Oil and gas push into gaps in rock

Reservoirs of oil and gas trapped by rocks

Global temperature changes

Connect the points (*) on this graph. The red line represents the average temperature in the mid-20th century. The points mark the differences between that temperature and the actual global temperature, taken every five years. Now answer the questions.

1. Which was the hottest year? ....

2. In which years was the temperature less than the average mid-20th century temperature?...

3. Did the temperature go up or down from 1995 to 2000?............................

4. Is the trend for global temperatures to get hotter or colder?........................

The rise in global temperature is causing the world's glaciers and ice sheets to melt more quickly.

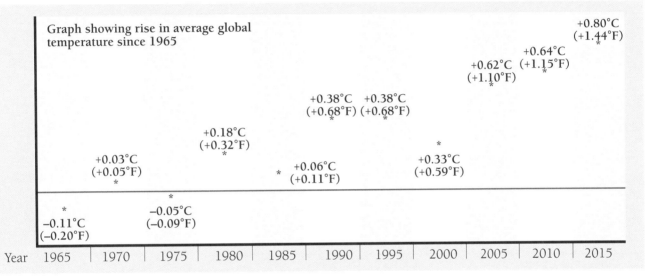

Graph showing rise in average global temperature since 1965

+0.80°C (+1.44°F)
+0.64°C (+1.15°F)
+0.62°C (+1.10°F)
+0.38°C (+0.68°F)   +0.38°C (+0.68°F)
+0.18°C (+0.32°F)
+0.03°C (+0.05°F)
+0.06°C (+0.11°F)
+0.33°C (+0.59°F)
−0.05°C (−0.09°F)
−0.11°C (−0.20°F)

Year 1965 1970 1975 1980 1985 1990 1995 2000 2005 2010 2015

Saving Earth's resources

Here are a few ways you can help save Earth's resources. For one week, fill in this chart by checking the relevant box each time you do something to help the planet.

Save water by turning off the tap while you brush your teeth.

Save fossil fuels, and prevent pollution, by leaving the car at home. Walk, ride your bike, or take public transportation when possible.

Save trees by writing on both sides of a piece of paper. Recycle the paper afterward instead of throwing it away.

Save land by taking your own carrier bags to the store. Landfill sites full of plastic bags and other rubbish use up too much of Earth's precious land.

Save the atmosphere by turning off lights and other electrical devices when not in use. This reduces the amount of fossil fuels burned to generate electricity. Also eat less meat, as livestock farming tends to increase the level of atmosphere-warming gases.

Earth and Its Structure

Check or number the boxes to answer each question. Check your answers on page 46.

1 From which direction does the Sun rise in the morning?

- ☐ **a.** North
- ☐ **b.** South
- ☐ **c.** East
- ☐ **d.** West

2 How long does it take Earth to make one complete orbit of the Sun?

- ☐ **a.** 365.26 days
- ☐ **b.** 366 days
- ☐ **c.** 24 hours
- ☐ **d.** 7 days

3 Number the layers of the atmosphere 1 to 4, in order from the ground up.

- ☐ **a.** Thermosphere
- ☐ **b.** Stratosphere
- ☐ **c.** Troposphere
- ☐ **d.** Mesosphere

4 Weather occurs in which layer of the atmosphere?

- ☐ **a.** Stratosphere
- ☐ **b.** Troposphere
- ☐ **c.** Thermosphere
- ☐ **d.** Mesosphere

5 The ozone layer is in which layer of the atmosphere?

- ☐ **a.** Troposphere
- ☐ **b.** Mesosphere
- ☐ **c.** Thermosphere
- ☐ **d.** Stratosphere

6 What keeps the atmosphere in place above Earth?

- ☐ **a.** Gravity
- ☐ **b.** Magnetism
- ☐ **c.** Heat
- ☐ **d.** Wind

7 What is the center of Earth called?

- ☐ **a.** Mantle
- ☐ **b.** Core
- ☐ **c.** Crust
- ☐ **d.** Atmosphere

8 The layer of Earth surrounding the mantle is called the:

- ☐ **a.** inner core
- ☐ **b.** atmosphere
- ☐ **c.** crust
- ☐ **d.** outer core

9 Which part of Earth's structure makes up nearly 84 percent of its volume?

- ☐ **a.** Core
- ☐ **b.** Mantle
- ☐ **c.** Crust
- ☐ **d.** Atmosphere

10 Check two metals found in Earth's core.

- ☐ **a.** Gold
- ☐ **b.** Iron
- ☐ **c.** Nickel
- ☐ **d.** Copper
- ☐ **e.** Titanium

11 The hole in the ozone layer is above which location?

- ☐ **a.** South Pole
- ☐ **b.** North Pole
- ☐ **c.** Equator
- ☐ **d.** Atlantic Ocean

Mountains, Volcanoes, and Earthquakes

Check or number the boxes to answer each question. Check your answers on page 46.

1 The point underground where rocks fracture and cause an earthquake is called:

- ☐ **a.** the focus
- ☐ **b.** the epicenter
- ☐ **c.** a seismic wave
- ☐ **d.** a rift valley

2 Check two characteristics of fold mountains.

- ☐ **a.** Tall
- ☐ **b.** Flat
- ☐ **c.** Rounded
- ☐ **d.** Rugged
- ☐ **e.** Smooth

3 Which of the following is a *not* a type of plate boundary?

- ☐ **a.** Divergent boundary
- ☐ **b.** Inverted boundary
- ☐ **c.** Transform fault
- ☐ **d.** Convergent boundary

4 What feature is caused by a transform fault?

- ☐ **a.** Volcano
- ☐ **b.** Mountain
- ☐ **c.** Earthquake
- ☐ **d.** Canyon

5 What is measured by the Mercalli scale?

- ☐ **a.** Effects of a volcano
- ☐ **b.** Altitude of a mountain
- ☐ **c.** Temperature of magma
- ☐ **d.** Effects of an earthquake

6 Pahoehoe is a type of:

- ☐ **a.** glacier
- ☐ **b.** lava
- ☐ **c.** crater
- ☐ **d.** volcanic mountain

7 Which of these are types of mountains?

- ☐ **a.** Volcano
- ☐ **b.** Round
- ☐ **c.** Fold
- ☐ **d.** Block

8 Number these events 1 to 4, in the order in which they occur in the formation of fold mountains.

- ☐ **a.** Weathering and erosion wear away the mountains.
- ☐ **b.** Over time, pressure causes the rocks to fold over, forming high mountain peaks.
- ☐ **c.** Two tectonic plates collide at a convergent boundary.
- ☐ **d.** Heat and pressure at the boundary cause rocks in the crust to buckle up.

9 What is the highest peak in the Alps?

- ☐ **a.** Mount Everest
- ☐ **b.** Mount Kosciuszko
- ☐ **c.** Mont Blanc
- ☐ **d.** Cerro Aconcagua

10 On which continent are the Rocky Mountains?

- ☐ **a.** South America
- ☐ **b.** Europe
- ☐ **c.** Africa
- ☐ **d.** North America

Rocks, Minerals, and Soil

Check or number the boxes to answer each question. Check your answers on page 46.

1 What are rocks made of?

- ☐ **a.** Soil
- ☐ **b.** Water
- ☐ **c.** Wood
- ☐ **d.** Minerals

2 Which of these is not a type of rock?

- ☐ **a.** Igneous
- ☐ **b.** Sedimentary
- ☐ **c.** Temperate
- ☐ **d.** Metamorphic

3 How can igneous rocks form?

- ☐ **a.** During earthquakes
- ☐ **b.** From the effects of heat or pressure
- ☐ **c.** From rock erosion
- ☐ **d.** When volcanic lava cools and hardens

4 Which type of rock is formed from small particles of eroded rock?

- ☐ **a.** Igneous
- ☐ **b.** Sedimentary
- ☐ **c.** Marble
- ☐ **d.** Metamorphic

5 Which of these is *not* a characteristic that helps identify a mineral?

- ☐ **a.** Crystal shape
- ☐ **b.** Color
- ☐ **c.** Noise
- ☐ **d.** Streak
- ☐ **e.** Hardness

6 Which characteristic of rocks is measured by Mohs' scale?

- ☐ **a.** Cleave
- ☐ **b.** Hardness
- ☐ **c.** Fracture
- ☐ **d.** Size of crystals

7 What is the top layer of soil made of?

- ☐ **a.** Humus
- ☐ **b.** Bedrock
- ☐ **c.** Weathered rock
- ☐ **d.** Metal

8 Check the two sedimentary rocks.

- ☐ **a.** Granite
- ☐ **b.** Marble
- ☐ **c.** Brecchia
- ☐ **d.** Gneiss
- ☐ **e.** Chalk

9 Igneous rocks usually have tightly interlocking crystals, so are generally:

- ☐ **a.** very soft
- ☐ **b.** very hard
- ☐ **c.** crumbly
- ☐ **d.** shiny

10 Which of these rocks is glossy and black, with very fine grains?

- ☐ **a.** Obsidian
- ☐ **b.** Gneiss
- ☐ **c.** Chalk
- ☐ **d.** Shale

11 Number these events 1 to 4, in the order in which they occur in the formation of fossils.

- ☐ **a.** The remains are buried by layers of sediment that gradually turn to rock.
- ☐ **b.** Over time, the rock is folded and eroded.
- ☐ **c.** Dead creatures sink into the seabed and rot.
- ☐ **d.** The fossils are eventually exposed on Earth's surface.

Earth, Water, and Ice

Check or number the boxes to answer each question. Check your answers on page 46.

1 What percentage of Earth's surface is covered by oceans?

- a. 10
- b. 30
- c. 70
- d. 90

2 Which is the world's largest ocean?

- a. Indian
- b. Atlantic
- c. Southern
- d. Pacific
- e. Arctic

3 Which of these forces causes ocean tides?

- a The magnetic pull between Earth and the Moon.
- b. The gravitational pull between Earth and the Moon.
- c. The flow of water from rivers to oceans.

4 What is a continental shelf?

- a. A flat area of sediment on the ocean floor
- b. An underwater volcano
- c. An undersea ledge that extends from the land
- d. An undersea slope

5 Check two sea creatures that live on the abyssal plain.

- a. Hatchet fish
- b. Brittlestar
- c. Tripod fish
- d. Coral

6 Number these river features in order, from 1 to 4, from the start of a river to the end.

- a. River source
- b. River mouth
- c. Meanders
- d. Rapids

7 What is a tributary?

- a. A curve in the lower reaches of the river
- b. A small stream or river that flows into a main river
- c. A type of waterfall
- d. A stretch of flat land beside a river that floods

8 The Yangtze River flows through which continent?

- a. Africa
- b. North America
- c. Asia
- d. Australia

9 Which of these rivers is the longest?

- a. Amazon
- b. Mississippi-Missouri
- c. Congo
- d. Nile

10 Snow that has been compressed to form a thick mass of ice is called a:

- a. caldera lake
- b. moraine
- c. glacier
- d. tarn

11 What happens when limestone rock comes into contact with water?

- a. Water dissolves the limestone, gradually forming a cave.
- b. The limestone holds the water like a sponge.
- c. The limestone prevents the water from seeping through.
- d. The water turns to ice.

Climate, Seasons, and Weather

Check or number the boxes to answer each question. Check your answers on page 46.

1 Where are dry areas usually located?

- [ ] a. Near the coast
- [ ] b. Inland, away from oceans
- [ ] c. Near the Equator
- [ ] d. At high altitudes

2 The climate in polar regions is:

- [ ] a. hot and humid
- [ ] b. cold and wet
- [ ] c. cold and dry
- [ ] d. seasonal

3 Stratus clouds are:

- [ ] a. wispy, high-altitude clouds
- [ ] b. fluffy white clouds
- [ ] c. billowing, gray rain clouds
- [ ] d. sheets of low-lying cloud

4 Water from oceans, lakes, and rivers evaporates into the air to form:

- [ ] a. clouds
- [ ] b. wind
- [ ] c. glaciers
- [ ] d. the ozone layer

5 Number these events 1 to 4, in the order they occur in the water cycle, beginning with rainfall.

- [ ] a. Clouds carry the water inland.
- [ ] b. Clouds release rain or snow onto the land.
- [ ] c. The rain collects in rivers and flows toward the ocean.
- [ ] d. Water evaporates from the oceans, lakes, and rivers to form clouds.

6 What does the Beaufort scale measure?

- [ ] a. Amount of rainfall
- [ ] b. Amount of sunshine
- [ ] c. Amount of snowfall
- [ ] d. Wind force

7 How many sides does a snowflake have?

- [ ] a. 4
- [ ] b. 5
- [ ] c. 6
- [ ] d. 7

8 During winter, the Sun is at:

- [ ] a. its highest point in the sky
- [ ] b. its lowest point in the sky
- [ ] c. the midpoint in the sky
- [ ] d. the Equator

9 When does the longest day of the year occur?

- [ ] a. Spring
- [ ] b. Summer
- [ ] c. Fall
- [ ] d. Winter

10 When do the North and South Poles get sunlight both day and night?

- [ ] a. Spring
- [ ] b. Summer
- [ ] c. Fall
- [ ] d. Winter

Features, Habitats, and Resources

Check or number the boxes to answer each question. Check your answers on page 46.

1 Which is the world's largest lake?
- ☐ a. Lake Erie
- ☐ b. Caspian Sea
- ☐ c. Lake Victoria
- ☐ d. Great Bear Lake

2 The Amazon rainforest is the world's largest:
- ☐ a. tropical forest
- ☐ b. temperate forest
- ☐ c. wetland
- ☐ d. woodland

3 Which is the world's largest desert?
- ☐ a. Atacama Desert
- ☐ b. Gobi Desert
- ☐ c. Great Sandy Desert
- ☐ d. Sahara Desert

4 On which continent does Uluru (Ayers Rock) lie?
- ☐ a. Antarctica
- ☐ b. Europe
- ☐ c. Australia
- ☐ d. North America

5 Tropical forests are home to what percentage of the world's plant and animal species?
- ☐ a. 10
- ☐ b. 25
- ☐ c. more than 40
- ☐ d. 80

6 Which habitat is dry because the ice there does not evaporate?
- ☐ a. Mountains
- ☐ b. Polar regions
- ☐ c. Temperate forest
- ☐ d. Desert

7 Bighorn sheep are well adapted for:
- ☐ a. swimming across rivers
- ☐ b. running fast
- ☐ c. walking easily over sand
- ☐ d. climbing mountains

8 In which habitat do alligators and crocodiles live?
- ☐ a. Polar regions
- ☐ b. Mountains
- ☐ c. Rivers and wetlands
- ☐ d. Desert

9 Which animal lives in a grassland habitat?
- ☐ a. Woodpecker
- ☐ b. Monkey
- ☐ c. Desert hamster
- ☐ d. Wildebeest

10 Check all the things that are Earth's natural resources.
- ☐ a. Water
- ☐ b. Plastic
- ☐ c. Fossil fuels
- ☐ d. Trees
- ☐ e. Atmosphere

11 Which of these actions will *not* help save Earth's resources?
- ☐ a. Turning off the water while you brush your teeth
- ☐ b. Leaving the lights on all night
- ☐ c. Taking your own carrier bag to the store
- ☐ d. Recycling paper

Activity Answers

Once you have completed each page of activities, check your answers below.

Page 14
Time test
1 Sun
2 Earth
3 east
4 rotation
5 Moon
6 366

Page 14
Which season?
1 Spring
2 Winter
3 Summer
4 Fall

Page 15
Atmospheric layers
1 Thermosphere
2 Mesosphere
3 Stratosphere
4 Troposphere

Page 15
True or false?
1 True
2 False—The thermosphere merges with space.
3 False—Weather occurs in the troposphere.
4 True
5 False—The hole in the ozone layer is above the South Pole.
6 True

Page 16
Inside the Earth
1 Inner core
2 Outer core
3 Mantle
4 Crust
5 Atmosphere

Page 17
Which boundary?
1 transform fault
2 divergent boundary
3 convergent boundary
4 transform fault

Page 17
Measuring earthquakes
a 10
b 3
c 6

Page 18
Fiery mountains
1 magma chamber
2 vents
3 lava
4 ash

Page 18
Volcano picture puzzle
1 Obsidian
2 Volcanic crater
3 Cinder cones
4 Pahoehoe

Page 19
True or false?
1 True
2 False—Fold mountains form when rocks fold over.
3 False—Fold mountains have high peaks.
4 True
5 False—Younger mountains generally have taller, sharper peaks than older ones.
6 True

Page 19
Mountain quiz
1 Mount Everest
2 Himalayas
3 Africa
4 Mont Blanc
5 4,470 miles (7,200 km)
6 Rocky Mountains

Pages 20 and 21
Natural wonders of the world
World's highest waterfall: Angel Falls
World's largest tropical forest: Amazon
World's largest ice sheet: Antarctic
World's largest desert: Sahara
World's largest lake: Caspian Sea
World's largest ocean: Pacific

Page 22
Rock cycle puzzle

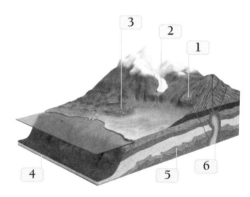

Page 22
Rocky landscapes
1 metamorphic
2 igneous
3 sedimentary

Page 23
Mineral test
1 streak
2 light
3 shape
4 breaks
5 diamond
6 softer

Page 23
How fossils form

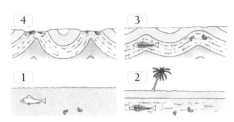

Page 24
Grain-size puzzle
1 medium
2 coarse
3 fine

Pages 24 and 25
Match the rocks and minerals
1 d Galena
2 c Gniess
3 e Obsidian
4 a Chalk
5 b Ruby

Page 26
On the ocean floor
1 Continental slope
2 Abyssal plain
3 Spreading ridge
4 Guyot

Page 26
Ocean quiz
1 toward
2 Moon
3 neap
4 crest
5 surface

Page 27
Match the coastline

Page 28
River features puzzle
1 rapids
2 meanders
3 waterfall
4 floodplain

Page 28
Follow the rivers

Nile
River source: Lake Victoria
River mouth: Mediterranean Sea
Flow direction: north

Amazon
River source: Andes Mountains
River mouth: Atlantic Ocean
Flow direction: east

Volga
River source: Valdai Hills
River mouth: Caspian Sea
Flow direction: south

Page 29
Lake formations
1 inland
2 caldera lakes
3 oxbow
4 glaciers

Page 29
True or false?
1 True
2 False—As sediment fills a lake, the water volume decreases.
3 True
4 True
5 False—Floodplains may become wetlands during the rainy season.

Page 30
Inside a cave

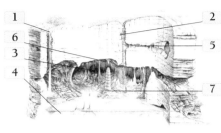

Page 31
The glacial landscape
1 U-shaped
2 tarn
3 moraine
4 hanging valley

Page 31
Arctic or Antarctic?
1 Antarctic
2 Arctic
3 Antarctic
4 Arctic
5 Antarctic

Page 32
Animal adaptations
Rivers and wetlands crocodiles, swimming
Tropical forest tails, rainforest
Polar regions fat, blubber
Mountains sheep, steep
Desert fur, sand
Temperate forest beaks, tree
Grassland digesting, grassland

Page 33
The water cycle

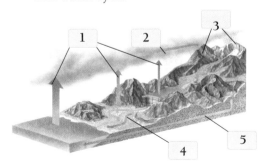

45

Answers

Page 33
Cloud puzzle
1 cumulus
2 cirrus
3 cumulonimbus
4 stratus

Page 34
Wind force puzzle
1 Wind force 6
2 Wind force 8
3 Wind force 3
4 Wind force 9

Page 36
True or false?
1 True
2 False—Increasing temperatures

cause sea levels to rise.
3 False—Burning fossil fuels releases
an excess of carbon dioxide into the
atmosphere.
4 True
5 True

Page 36
Fossil fuels puzzle
1 Dead organisms fall to the ocean
floor.
2 Sediment compresses the remains
of organisms to form oil and
natural gas.
3 Oil and gas push into the
surrounding rock.
4 Over time, other rocks trap the oil
and gas in underground reservoirs.

Page 37
Global temperature changes

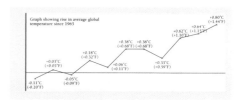

1 2015
2 1965 and 1975
3 down
4 hotter

Quick Quiz Answers

Once you have completed each page of quiz questions,
check your answers below.

Page 38
Earth and Its Structure
1 c 2 a 3 a4, b2, c1, d3 4 b 5 d 6 a
7 b 8 c 9 b 10 b, c 11 a

Page 39
**Mountains, Volcanoes, and
Earthquakes**
1 a 2 a, d 3 b 4 c 5 d 6 b 7 a, c, d
8 a4, b3, c1, d2 9 c 10 d

Page 40
Rocks, Minerals, and Soil
1 d 2 c 3 d 4 b 5 c 6 b 7 a 8 c, e
9 b 10 a 11 a2, b3, c1, d4

Page 41
Earth, Water, and Ice
1 c 2 d 3 b 4 c 5 b, c
6 a1, b4, c3, d2 7 b 8 c 9 d 10 c
11 a

Page 42
Climate, Seasons, and Weather
1 b 2 c 3 d 4 a 5 a4, b1, c2, d3 6 d
7 c 8 b 9 b 10 b

Page 43
Features, Habitats, and Resources
1 b 2 a 3 d 4 c 5 c 6 b 7 d 8 c
9 d 10 a, c, d, e 11 b

Acknowledgments

The publisher would like to thank
the following:

Alyson Silverwood for proofreading,
Robert Dinwiddie for 2020 consultant
review, and Harish Aggarwal and
Priyanka Sharma for the jacket.

The publisher would like to thank the
following for their kind permission to
reproduce their photographs:

(Key: a-above; b-below/bottom; c-centre;
l-left; r-right; t-top)

DK Images: Ironbridge Gorge Museum,
Telford, Shropshire 38bc, National Trust
20; Natural History Museum, London
9cb, 18br, 39cra.

All other images © Dorling Kindersley
For further information see:
www.dkimages.com

MAJOR RIVERS

NAME	NILE	AMAZON	YANGTZE
LOCATION	AFRICA	SOUTH AMERICA	ASIA
LENGTH	6,650 KM (4,132 MILES)	6,575 KM (4,085 MILES)	6,300 KM (3,915 MILES)
SOURCE	LAKE VICTORIA	ANDES MOUNTAINS	HIMALAYAS
RIVER MOUTH	MEDITERRANEAN SEA	ATLANTIC OCEAN	EAST CHINA SEA

NAME	MISSISSIPPI–MISSOURI	CONGO	VOLGA
LOCATION	NORTH AMERICA	AFRICA	EUROPE
LENGTH	6,275 KM (3,900 MILES)	4,700 KM (2,920 MILES)	3,645 KM (2,265 MILES)
SOURCE	LAKE ITASCA, MINNESOTA	EAST AFRICAN PLATEAU	VALDAI HILLS, RUSSIAN FEDERATION
RIVER MOUTH	GULF OF MEXICO	ATLANTIC OCEAN	CASPIAN SEA

MAJOR MOUNTAIN RANGES

NAME	ATLAS	ALPS	GREAT DIVIDING RANGE
LOCATION	AFRICA	EUROPE	AUSTRALIA
RANGE LENGTH	2,400 KM (1,500 MILES)	1,050 KM (650 MILES)	3,600 KM (2,250 MILES)
HIGHEST PEAK	TOUBKAL	MONT BLANC	MT. KOSCIUSZKO
PEAK HEIGHT	4,167 M (13,671 FT)	4,808 M (15,774 FT)	2,228 M (7,310 FT)

NAME	ANDES	ROCKY MOUNTAINS	HIMALAYAS
LOCATION	SOUTH AMERICA	NORTH AMERICA	ASIA
RANGE LENGTH	7,200 KM (4,470 MILES)	6,000 KM (3,700 MILES)	2,600 KM (1,600 MILES)
HIGHEST PEAK	CERRO ACONCAGUA	MT ELBERT	MOUNT EVEREST (WORLD'S HIGHEST MOUNTAIN)
PEAK HEIGHT	6,961 M (22,838 FT)	4,401 M (14,439 FT)	8,848 M (29,029 FT)

EARTH RECORD BREAKERS

RECORD	HEAVIEST RAIN IN 24 HOURS	WETTEST PLACE	DRIEST PLACE
STATISTICS	RAINFALL 71.9 IN (1,825 MM)	ANNUAL RAINFALL 467½ IN (11,872 MM)	ANNUAL RAINFALL 1/250 IN (0.1 MM)
LOCATION	REUNION ISLAND, INDIAN OCEAN	MAWSYNRAM, INDIA	ATACAMA DESERT, CHILE
CONTINENT	AFRICA	ASIA	SOUTH AMERICA
CLIMATE ZONE	TROPICAL	TROPICAL	DRY

RECORD	HIGHEST RECORDED TEMPERATURE	LOWEST RECORDED TEMPERATURE	WINDIEST PLACE
STATISTICS	TEMPERATURE 134.1°F (56.7°C)	TEMPERATURE −128°F (−89°C)	HIGHEST DAILY AVERAGE 108 MPH (174 KPH)
LOCATION	DEATH VALLEY, CALIFORNIA	VOSTOK RESEARCH STATION	PORT MARTIN
CONTINENT	NORTH AMERICA	ANTARCTICA	ANTARCTICA
CLIMATE ZONE	DRY	POLAR	POLAR

RECORD	HIGHEST WATERFALL	LARGEST OCEAN	LARGEST LAKE
STATISTICS	HEIGHT 3,212 FT (979 M)	AREA 64 MILLION SQ MILES (165 MILLION SQ KM)	AREA 143,205 SQ MILES (371,000 SQ KM)
NAME	ANGEL FALLS	PACIFIC OCEAN	CASPIAN SEA
FEATURES	CASCADES DOWN AUYAN TEPUI, VENEZUELA	DEEPEST POINT MARIANA TRENCH	LANDLOCKED SALTWATER LAKE
LOCATION	SOUTH AMERICA	COVERS 1/3 OF EARTH'S SURFACE	ASIA

RECORD	LARGEST TROPICAL FOREST	LARGEST DESERT	LARGEST ICE SHEET
STATISTICS	AREA 2.1 MILLION SQ MILES (5.5 MILLION SQ KM)	AREA 3.5 MILLION SQ MILES (9 MILLION SQ KM)	AREA 5.3 MILLION SQ MILES (13.7 MILLION SQ KM)
NAME	AMAZON RAINFOREST	SAHARA DESERT	ANTARCTIC ICE SHEET
FEATURES	GREATEST VARIETY OF WILDLIFE ON EARTH	SAND DUNES AND STRONG WINDS	EXTENDS INTO SOUTHERN OCEAN
LOCATION	SOUTH AMERICA	NORTH AFRICA	ANTARCTICA